WISDOM TREE

Contents

1. **Justice**   3
   At his best, man is the noblest of all animals; separated from law and justice he is the worst.

2. **Value for National and Civic Property**   11
   Respect and value national and civic property.

My Guiding Principles

3. **Quest for Knowledge**   19
   Knowledge is Power. Keep Reading.

4. **Self-Discipline**   27
   With self-discipline, almost anything is possible.

5. **Valuing Time**   35
   Lost time is never found again.

A Collage of Values

7. **Sympathy**   46
   Shared joy is a double joy; shared sorrow is half a sorrow.

My Declaration

Justice

Justice is being fair. It is being impartial. It is ensuring that everyone gets an equal chance at things. It is ensuring that everyone gets the share of things that they deserve. It is ensuring that no one gets cheated.

Read the following story to better understand the concept of and need for justice.

The Story

This is the story of Prince Lapio, a wayward prince, who was taught in a very clever way about justice.

Intelligent, courageous and handsome, Prince Lapio looked like he had all the qualities to become a king. However, not every person can be perfect. The prince had no sense of justice. If ever there was a dispute, he would take the side of the person who could talk more convincingly or who looked more handsome and well dressed. This is not the way justice is served.

How then do you think the prince learnt about justice? It happened quite by chance when he was shipwrecked. He and another person were the only survivors; they ended up on an uninhabited island. So they both decided to stick together to reach their country safely.

The prince was good at fishing. He was always successful in catching himself fish to eat. He, however, refused to share the fish with his fellow survivor. The other person, a wise old man, then thought of a clever way of catching birds. Thus, he too had his share of food and did not starve.

One day, the prince hurt himself and was unable to walk down to the beach to hunt. He was hungry. He asked the old man to give him some of the birds to eat. The old man refused. "You did not want to share your fish with me, and now you expect me to share my bird with you. I think I will not."

The poor prince was not used to stay hungry. He soon grew weak and frustrated. He finally said, "I am sorry that I did not want to share my food with you. I have learnt my lesson. Justice is in sharing what you have equally."

The old man smiled and shared his food with the prince. This went on for some days. The prince recovered and he shared the fish he caught from then on.

Many days passed and finally a passing ship rescued the two of them. On board the ship was a chief of a tribe. He looked worried. The prince asked him what was troubling him. The chief replied, "My neighbouring tribe and mine own some land together. We till the land and harvest the fields together. However, when it comes to sharing the crop, we always end up fighting.

The prince said, "I have recently learnt that you should share whatever you have equally. So divide the food into two equal portions. You take one and give the other to the neighbouring tribe."

The village chief was not happy with this reply. He said, "But the people of my tribe are tall and need more food. The people of my neighbouring tribe are pygmies and do not need as much food. If I divide the food equally, my tribe will not have enough food. They will lose their energy and eventually starve while the other tribe will have sumptuous food which will eventually go waste."

The prince thought for a while and said, "Don't share the food equally. Instead, see how much food each person in both the tribes needs and distribute it accordingly. Dispense food according to their need."

This sounded better. The chief thanked the prince. On reaching the shore, they both went their separate ways. The old man was however still with the prince. He too had to reach the prince's city and so they both decided to travel together. They had now become good friends.

The prince said, "On this journey, I have learnt that while it is just to share, we should also take into account people's needs while sharing or distributing."

Finally, the two reached a village on the outskirts of their kingdom. Here, the prince declared who he was and asked if anyone could give him and his companion horses to ride back to his castle. A poor village blacksmith, who was dressed in tatters, offered his only horse to the prince. The village headman, a wealthy merchant also offered his finest horse to the prince. In addition, he also offered some food for the way and ordered a few of his personal soldiers to accompany the prince to the castle.

The prince was happy with the help offered. He and the old man reached the castle in safety and in comfort. He wanted to now pay back the two people from the village that had helped with horses. He had two bags of gold brought. He saw to it that one bag had more gold than the other. He ordered the bag with more gold to be given to the poor blacksmith. The bag with the lesser amount of gold was to be given to the village headman.

The old man asked the prince why he had not distributed the gold equally. The prince replied, "The village headman spent more money on me. He gave me his finest horse, and also spared some of his soldiers to accompany me. However, the blacksmith gave me his only possession, his horse. The village headman has more horses and more servants and soldiers with him. However, the blacksmith had nothing more left with him and yet he was willing to give what he had."

What I realized from this trip is that one should share, while taking into account the needs of the people as well as the merit of the person receiving the share. This, according to me, is true justice.

Test your understanding of the story. Answer the questions.

1. What were the prince's merits and what was his flaw?
   _____
   _____

2. Before getting shipwrecked, how did the prince settle any dispute?
   _____
   _____

3. What was the first lesson about justice that the prince learnt after getting hurt on the island?
   _____
   _____

4. What made the prince change his idea of justice after listening to the tribal chief's story?
   _____
   _____

5. Why did the prince decide to give the bag with more gold to the blacksmith instead of the village headman?
   _____
   _____

6. What did the prince learn about justice at the end?
   _____
   _____

More about the value

We have courts, judges and lawyers to ensure justice. It is their duty to make sure that people get the share of what they deserve. It is their duty to ensure that people are not cheated or exploited.

However, we should not leave justice only to the hands of a lawyer or a judge. Each one of us has to inculcate the value of justice. We should behave in such a way that we never cheat others. At the same time, we should look out that we are not cheated either.

How often do you say, "It is not fair!" Every time you say that, remember that you feel justice is not met. When you want justice, you should also see to it that others around you also have justice.

For instance, a boy from your cricket team is being given a chance to continue batting even though he was caught out. This is because he is much younger than the other players in the group. So, most of the players have decided that this younger kid would be given two chances at the wicket. If you feel that this is injustice, imagine yourself playing with much older people. Wouldn't you be made out easily by them? Wouldn't you want to have two chances to bat while playing with them?

Put yourself in the other person's shoes and think whether what you feel is justified or not.

If every one of us strives to be just, the world will be a beautiful place.

A VALUE FOR ME

At his best, man is the noblest of all animals; separated from law and justice he is the worst.

Snippet

On their parents' death, two brothers were to inherit their father's property. The younger brother was a meek fellow. He never could say no to anybody, especially his older brother.

The older brother was just the opposite to him. Knowing that his brother would never argue about anything, he took it on himself to divide the property. He ensured that he got all the fields that were near the pond, making it easy for the fields to be irrigated. He decided to give away those fields that were far from the pond to the younger brother.

Though the younger brother never argued for his rights, he was not foolish either. He realized that his brother was trying to cheat him. However, he did not know how to put forward his case and ask for an even distribution of the property.

He then approached the village headman, who was a wise old man. He came up with a solution. He called both the brothers. He told the elder brother to divide the property into two parts. But the choice of which part to take would be given to the younger brother. Whatever piece of the divided property he chose would be his. The other would belong to the older brother.

The older brother was in a fix. He was now forced to make a fair and equal distribution. Else, his younger brother could walk away with the better share.

Let Us Do

1. Though we all like to believe in fairness, life is not always fair. Have you ever felt that something done by someone was unfair? Describe the incident in the space below. Mention why you felt the incident was unfair and how you would rectify the situation to ensure justice.

   Across:

   _____
   _____
   _____
   _____
   _____
   _____
   _____

2. In which of the following situations has justice been meted out or which of them according to you are not fair?
   a. Gandhiji was not allowed on the first-class coach of a train because he was not a 'white'. _____
   b. In India, people are not discriminated on the basis of their language or religion. _____
   c. Seema and Naseem are not allowed to vote because they are not yet 18 years old. _____
   d. People of India cannot go abroad without a passport. _____
   e. While playing cricket, Gaurav hit the ball into the bushes. None of the boys could find the ball. It was Mahesh's ball and it was lost. Gaurav bought a new ball and handed it over to Mahesh. _____

3. **People should be given equal opportunities. Justice lies in giving equal opportunities to all to develop themselves. Let us learn this through an activity.** Get one pair of sharp scissors and another pair of blunt scissors. Now try to cut designs out of paper using blunt pair of scissors. After making around two designs, switch to the better pair of scissors. Make two more paper cuttings with this pair of scissors.

   Have you noticed any difference in the paper cuttings? Do you think you were able to make equally good paper cuttings using both the pairs of scissors?

Based on your experience with this activity, write a few lines on why you think equal opportunity is important to social justice?

_____
_____
_____
_____
_____
_____
_____

4. **Collect information about any one of the following people and write down how they had talked and tried to bring about social justice.**

   a. Mahatma Gandhi

   b. Martin Luther King

   _____
   _____
   _____
   _____
   _____

   Paste a picture of the person or draw the person in the space given here.

   _____
   _____
   _____

5. **Activity Time**

   We may look different, speak different languages, dress differently, but eventually, all humankind is the same from within. Let us learn this through an activity.

   Each student in the class will have to get one orange to school. If this is not the orange season, a lemon will also do. Before placing the oranges or the lemons in a basket (set up in a corner of the classroom), each of you will have to look at your fruit keenly. You may be able to find a mark or something on the fruit that will stand out on it. Once you place the fruit in the basket, you might still be able to identify your own fruit. The next day, all of you will peel the fruits. Put the fruit back in the basket. Now try to find your fruit. Are you able to identify your own fruit?

What have you learnt from this activity?

_____
_____
_____

* The activity aims to point out that people are alike. Therefore, they should not be discriminated against or given preferential treatment.

How much do you stand by justice? Test yourself.

1. Do you expect to be treated differently? Do you think you can expect others to listen to you and do as you say, but you will do only as you wish?
2. Do you think it is a good thing to lie?
3. Should you treat your friend or relative in a special way, while there are others?
4. Do you own up your mistakes and not pass the blame onto someone else?
5. Do you violate rules when you think that no one is looking?

* If your answers to questions 1, 2, 3 and 5 are 'yes', then you do not believe in justice.

Tips to Parents and Teachers

Teaching children that life isn't always fair is important. However, it is more important to teach them to stand by what is right, no matter what. Just because the world is unfair does not mean that we too become unfair. Children should be taught that change can begin with just one person – them.

Do's and Don'ts

1. Always speak the truth. Avoid lying.
2. Treat others the way you would want to be treated.
3. Follow rules, wherever you are.
4. Be considerate of others. Think about how your actions or words could affect other people.
5. Don't make special favours for friends or relatives. Treat everyone equally.
6. Never blame others for your mistakes.
7. Keep an open mind when listening to someone. Don't be prejudiced.

Value for National and Civic Property

We take care of our property. We like to keep our house clean. Similarly, we should take care of our national and civic property. We should keep them clean and avoid damaging them. National and civic property belong to everyone in the country. They belong to the country and to every one of us. We should take pride in them and also help maintain them.

Read the following story to better understand the concept of and need for justice.

Read and Think

India is an ancient land with many historic monuments of immense value. The Taj Mahal is the crowning glory, as it is a part of the new Seven Wonders of the World list. The others like the temples of Hampi, Konark, Tanjavur and Madurai, the Charminar and the Jama Masjid are just a few to name that are simply breathtaking.

The synagogue of Cochi, the Victoria Memorial at Kolkata, and the Gateway of India at Mumbai are memories of our contact with ancient cultures and the European nations and their influence on our country and its culture.

Still others like the caves of Bhimbhetka are reminiscent of the prehistoric times when people inhabited our country, while there are thousands of ruins that dot our country that tell silent stories of people's and culture's past.

The forts and palaces like the Hawa Mahal, the Amer Fort and many others stand testimony to our architectural feats and help us remember the kings who commissioned them.

These and many more that we can list here are impossible to replace if destroyed or damaged. Moreover, just as we take pride in showing a neat and well-decorated home to our visitors, we should take pride in showing a well-maintained country to the world.

While it is possible to make an estimate of how much money these monuments would need to be rebuilt in the current times, it is impossible to replicate their exquisiteness and their intricate craftsmanship.

Further, India is also a vast country with so many public and civic properties that their numbers can easily run into thousands if not more. The roads, pavements, public buildings, bridges like libraries, police stations and so on, dams, etc. are all part of civic property. While they belong to the government of India, they also belong to us, the people.

When we take such good care of our own car or cycle, why shouldn't we take care of our buses, trains and aircraft? Defacing the walls of monuments or tearing the seats because one is bored is not a good thing. We see that many people spit on the roads. This dirties our towns and cities.

Countries like Singapore have banned chewing gums to ensure that their country is neat. The Indian government spends crores of rupees in building civic property for our use. According to one estimate, it takes around Rs. 14 crore to build a kilometre long road. Imagine how much it takes to build all the civic property that we enjoy today.

What good would it do to damage them and then demand the government to rebuild these roads or buildings? Wouldn't the money spent in rebuilding or repairing be put to better use? We could have a new library building, a new park or a new road instead of rebuilding the existing one.

So the next time you are on the roads or in a public park or in a train, think of our country. Take pride in our national property and help keep them neat.

Test your understanding of the essay. Answer the questions.

1. What do you understand by national property?
   _____
   _____

2. What do you understand by civic property?
   _____
   _____

3. Name some of the historic monuments of our country that are listed in this essay.
   _____
   _____

4. Why according to this essay should we take care of our national and civic property? List as many points from the essay as you can.
   _____
   _____
   _____
   _____
   _____

5. Why does the author keep saying that national and civic property belongs to both the people and the country?
   _____
   _____

More about the value

Our country is one of those countries that allow much freedom to its citizens. We are free to reside anywhere in our country; we are free to practice any profession we wish; we are free to follow any religion we like; we are free to voice our opinion. Not many countries provide such freedom.

We are also blessed to be in a country that has immense national, historical and civic property. It is our responsibility as a citizen of this country to ensure that the country's property is safeguarded, maintained and kept from any kind of damage. This is our civic responsibility.

A VALUE FOR ME

Respect and value national and civic property.

Snippet

India is an ancient land with centuries of history reflected in its monuments, people and their culture. In such a vast nation as ours, there are innumerable monuments of national pride. Also, a developing nation such as ours with a huge population that needs to be benefitted from the natural and civic resources of the country, it is in our interest to safeguard our national property.

12th January has been declared as the Heritage Day in our country. Children in all schools across the country are advised to take the following oath.

I am proud of the rich culture and heritage of India.

I will respect all monuments which are a part of my country's heritage.

I will not scribble, deface or encroach upon any monument.

I pledge to render all possible help to conserve and preserve our heritage.

I along with my school mates will endeavour to save and protect the heritage site at (……………………………………………)

(Name of identified local heritage site)

Let Us Do

1. **Which of the following would you consider as public property? Put a tick mark against your answers.**

    Public libraries ☐

    Parks ☐

    Stadiums ☐

    Roads ☐

    Hospitals ☐

    Government offices ☐

Electric poles and electric wires on the road ☐

Post boxes ☐

Public transport ☐

Reserved forests ☐

2. Activity Time

Take up any one public property of your choice. For instance, you could choose the railways, the roads or the public parks. Make a list of at least 6 points that instruct people how to ensure that the public property is maintained, used properly and not damaged. Make copies of these and distribute them at the public space of your choice.

It's our property. Let's take care of it.

_____
_____
_____
_____
_____
_____

3. Imagine you are the Prime Minister of our country. Write a speech that you would deliver to the nation over the radio about the need to take care of national and civic properties.

_____
_____
_____
_____
_____
_____
_____
_____

Do you care for national and civic property? Test yourself. Which of the following points do you agree with?

1. You like to keep your surrounding neat and tidy because you love your community. You want everyone in your community to enjoy the neat space.
2. Since there are people to clean up public spaces like parks and roads, you need not really be bothered about keeping them clean. After all, if no one dirties the roads or the buildings, there would be no need for janitors to take care of that aspect. The janitors would be out of job.
3. A penny saved is a penny earned. If we take care not to vandalize our public property, we need not spend additional money on their repair, and thereby ours will be a richer community; a richer country.
4. Taking care of national and civic property is the responsibility of every citizen of this country.
5. We should take care of national and civic property because if we are caught destroying it or causing it harm in any way, we could be jailed.

* *If you agree with points 1, 3 and 4, you are sensitive not only to others in your society, but are also a responsible citizen.*

Tips to Parents and Teachers

Parents can talk to children from a very young age about how vandalism or any kind of damage to public property through dirtying, disfiguring or graffiti on them is not acceptable. Point out how much of government money, which in turn is tax payers' money, is spent in building or repairing them. Encourage children to respect their environment and all public property. Set an example and lead the way.

Dos and Don'ts

1. Put any waste only in a dustbin.
2. If you don't find a dustbin nearby, keep the object aside till you find a dustbin.
3. Never spit chewing gum on the road or stick it on the walls of buildings.
4. If you find anyone spitting betel leaves onto the roads or the walls of buildings, tell them politely not to do so.
5. Never write on walls, buses and trains and so on. Remember that it takes a lot to repaint them.
6. When visiting a park, take care not to trample on the bushes and plants in it.
7. Flowers on trees are for all to enjoy. Don't go plucking them in a public park.

My Guiding Principles

Here is a list of values. Be honest and sort them into the table below. On the next page, write down the time when you showed these principles.

(Caring)   (Patient)   (Forgiving)   (Courageous)

(Truthful)   (Fair)   (Honest)

(Helpful)   (Kind)

I am	I need to be

My Journal of Values

The time when I was _____ (insert a value here)

_____
_____
_____
_____
_____
_____
_____
_____
_____
_____
_____
_____

The time when I was _____ (insert a value here)

_____
_____
_____
_____
_____
_____
_____
_____
_____
_____
_____
_____

Quest for Knowledge

Information, facts and skills that are acquired by reading as well as through practical experiences are called knowledge. Quest for knowledge is a search for this knowledge. It is a long and continuous process. Knowledge is important for our growth, comfort and also for a pleasant life.

Read the following brief biography to better understand the need for every person to seek knowledge.

The Story

Thomas Edison, a name famously associated with the light bulb, had invented the incandescent lamp. He was a keen inventor. During his lifetime, he had filed more than 1,500 patents. A patent is a permission given legally to use, make or sell an invention. This means that Edison had the right over 1,500 inventions, all of which he had painstakingly done. If anyone wanted to use them or remake what he had invented, they had to take Edison's permission.

Edison was not merely an inventor. He was also a businessman. In his lifetime, he had established 14 companies, one of which is the famous GE.

For such an outstanding person, inventor and successful businessman, you would have thought that he was very well educated and hardworking. All this he was. However, what is stunning about Edison apart from his numerous patents and companies is that he was homeschooled! He was almost entirely educated at home and not in a school.

As a child, he was very easily distracted. Therefore, just three months after he started formal school, he was asked to leave. From then on, he studied at home and never went to any other school. He was mostly taught by his mother at home.

Well, homeschooling does not actually sound all that astounding, does it? As long as you have someone to teach you well at home, and you have the necessary books and material to study from, a homeschooled person could also excel in life.

But here is another interesting fact about Edison that would make his ability to make outstanding inventions seem greater than they already are. Edison had nearly lost hearing at a young age. He was almost deaf, with very little hearing capacity. Do you think that this handicap would affect a person's ability to learn?

Many might be demotivated by this handicap, but not Edison. Partial deafness did not deter his quest for knowledge. He was always hungry for more knowledge.

Apart from his yearning to learn and learn more, he was also extremely innovative. He was an entrepreneur. He sold candy and newspapers on trains when very young to earn himself money. Once, while at the railway station selling newspapers, he saved a telegrapher's son from being run over by a train. Out of gratitude and on recognizing that Edison was a bright and educated boy, the man gave Edison a job as a telegrapher at the station.

Edison worked very hard here. He worked for 12 hours a day, and six days a week. He worked during the nights so that he could continue to read and experiment during the day. He was always searching for knowledge and trying to discover or invent something. All of this – his quest for knowledge and a yearning to do something new, paid off.

Today and for all posterity, Thomas Alva Edison will be remembered as a genius inventor and entrepreneur, the inventor of the phonograph, the stock ticker, the fluoroscope, the kinetoscope and most importantly of all, the first commercially successful incandescent lamp.

> Edison was known as the 'Wizard of Menlo Park.'

Test your understanding of the biography. Answer the questions.

1. What is Thomas Alva Edison most famous for?
   _____
   _____

2. What are the two stunning facts about Edison that make him appear an even greater genius than he is?
   _____
   _____

3. Explain why the author says that despite his handicap, Edison's quest of knowledge made him the great person that he is.

_____

_____

4. Why did Edison prefer to work at nights, even though he had to work 12 hours a day?

_____

_____

5. What did Schmuel eventually realize?

_____

_____

6. Mention at least two qualities that you find in Edison that helped him to gain more knowledge?

_____

_____

More about the value

It is said that

Learning is the beginning of wealth.

Learning is the beginning of health.

Learning is the beginning of spirituality.

Human beings are curious by nature. Right from when they are born, people are curious about things and how they work. A baby learns how to walk, talk, hold things and use them only because of the curiosity. Curiosity leads to gaining knowledge.

But gaining knowledge should not be limited to only learning the basics of life. Do you think it is enough if you knew how to cook and hold a spoon so that you could eat?

Learning has to be a continuous process. What is today might change tomorrow. We need to learn so that we can cope with tomorrow and the surprises that it brings. Unless we learn and are prepared, we will not be able to live a content, happy, healthy and safe life.

Spend your time in gaining knowledge, and you would spent your time wisely. You may not realize it, but there is an opportunity to learn something new every second of your life. Learning should be quest. You should not stop the process till the day you die.

A VALUE FOR ME
Knowledge is power. Keep Reading.

Snippet

Have you heard of the story of the two friends who encounter a bear in the forest?

Once there were two friends walking through a forest. They heard a bear growling from somewhere nearby. Fearing for their lives, they thought of what they could do to save themselves. One of the boys scrambled up a tree, as high as he could. He knew that bears could not climb trees, so he should be safe.

The other boy, sadly, could not climb trees. He tried a lot of times, but he could not hoist himself up, nor was his friend anywhere in sight to help him. His friend had already climbed high up the tree to save himself.

The only other alternative that struck the boy was to lie as still as possible on the forest floor, pretending to be asleep.

Though it was dangerous, it was a trick that might save him from the bear. And it worked! The bear mistook the boy to be dead and left him be.

You see, bears are not scavengers. They generally do not eat dead things.

If you have heard this story earlier, you would also have learnt its moral – A friend in need is a friend indeed. The boy who left his friend when they were faced by danger wasn't really a good friend. He should have stayed back to help his friend climb the tree as well.

Can you think of the other value you can glean out of this story? The boy who lay down on the forest floor knew of a fact that bears mostly do not bother with dead beings. This knowledge came to his rescue.

Knowledge never goes waste, provided you are able to recall it at the apt moment.

Let Us Do

1. How do you gain knowledge? What are the various sources from which you acquire knowledge. List them out and paste pictures of the same.

2. Knowledge never goes waste. In the same breath, it is wise to remember that time gone by is time lost forever. Therefore, spend every minute you can in a profitable way. Gaining knowledge is one way of making good use of time.

    Gaining knowledge can affect your personality. Identify words in the word grid to fill in the blanks in the sentences below. All these sentences indicate how you become a better person by gaining knowledge.

    a. You grow _____.

    b. You are _____ to face life.

    c. You can tackle _____ with more confidence and more effectively.

A	P	B	V	M	M	V	U	C
P	R	E	P	A	R	E	D	O
H	O	R	Y	D	C	U	R	B
U	B	V	G	W	D	T	X	K
Y	L	T	R	D	I	D	C	S
E	E	R	Q	H	T	S	Z	A
T	M	A	Y	U	I	O	E	E
G	S	S	W	G	Y	H	Z	R

3. Name any eight books that you have read. Mention any one thing that you learnt (either a new word, a new fact, or a new value) from each of these books.

Sl. No.	Book that I have read	New thing that I have learnt from this book
1.		
2.		
3.		
4.		
5.		
6.		
7.		
8.		

4. Which of the following activities do you indulge in?

   a. Read books other than your school books

   b. Listen to music

   c. Learn new songs

   d. Dance

e. Play sports

f. Participate in plays

g. Travel to new places

h. Visit museums

i. Taste new varieties of foods

j. Solve puzzles

All these activities help you in gaining knowledge.

5. **When you see, read or hear of something, remember to ask questions. You don't have to ask others the answers. When you ask yourself questions, and then try to get the answers to these questions, you will gain knowledge.**

For instance, you see a bird in the sky, ask yourself,

a. How can birds fly?

b. Why cannot humans fly?

c. What helps the birds to fly?

d. When can humans fly?

e. Where are the birds flying to?

Get answers to these questions and you are a wiser person.

Now figure out something that interests you. Then ask questions relating to this. Find out the answers too. See how much you have learnt by the end of this exercise.

a. How _____

b. What _____

c. Why _____

d. When _____

e. Where _____

Write your answers here:

_____
_____
_____
_____

Do you seek knowledge or do you shy away from it? Test yourself.

1. Do you like reading books apart from those prescribed in your school?
2. Do you like to follow the news on TV or do you look forward to reading any newspaper or magazine?
3. Do you like learning new things – games, arts or even words from other languages?
4. Do you like talking to new people and making them friends?
5. Do you hate surprises? Do you want things to be the same always?

   *If your answers to all the above questions except the last one are 'yes' then you are keen on gaining knowledge.

Tips to Parents and Teachers

Remember that you are your child's best teacher. School, educational games and television, and a shelf full of books can't accomplish what you can in the education of your child. It doesn't take much effort to inspire a child's brain in the everyday world - the place where they need it the most. Here are a few simple things you can do to engage your child: count the number of houses, black cars, bicycles, etc. that you pass as you drive; search for letters, numbers, or colors on the restaurant menu; when you are going to use a gum-ball machine, hold out a handful of coins and explain the differences, and that the machine will only take the quarter (then let your child pick out a quarter and put it in the machine - they love this!).

Do's and Don'ts

1. Practice or recollect what you have already learnt.
2. Don't be shy to ask questions when you don't know about something. Asking questions and getting answers to them is the simplest way of gaining knowledge.
3. Be grateful for the chance you have to gain knowledge. Grab the opportunity.
4. Don't be afraid of trying new things. But make sure that what you are doing is safe.
5. Spread knowledge. The more you teach others what you know, the more you share your knowledge with others, the more you will learn.
6. Books are called the windows to the world. Make reading a habit. The more you read, the more knowledge you gain.
7. Keep your eyes and ears open. See things. Observe them keenly. Hear things. Listen well.
8. Finally, write down what you have learnt. It will help you to remember better.

Self-Discipline

When you are angry and you are able to control it, you have self-discipline. If you are hungry but have to wait till the bell rings to indicate that it is lunch break, before you open your box, you have self-discipline. Though you don't like doing something, for instance, you may not like exercising, but you do it nevertheless, because you know that it is good for your health, you have self-discipline.
Self-discipline is the ability to control one's emotions and overcome any weakness. Self-discipline is the ability to be disciplined by yourself, without someone else like a parent, a teacher or a law telling you.
Self-discipline comes from within. It is not enforced by someone else.

Read the following poem to better understand the need, importance and benefits of being self-disciplined.

Read and Think

The Ant and The Cricket

- Anonymous

A silly young cricket, accustomed to sing
Through the warm, sunny months of gay summer and spring,
Began to complain, when he found that at home
His cupboard was empty and winter was come.

Not a crumb to be found
On the snow-covered ground;
Not a flower could he see,
Not a leaf on a tree.
"Oh, what will become," says the cricket, "of me?"
At last by starvation and famine made bold,
All dripping with wet and all trembling with cold,
Away he set off to a miserly ant
To see if, to keep him alive, he would grant
Him shelter from rain.

A mouthful of grain
He wished only to borrow,
He'd repay it tomorrow;
If not helped, he must die of starvation and sorrow.
Says the ant to the cricket: "I'm your servant and friend,
But we ants never borrow, we ants never lend.

Please tell me, dear sir, did you lay nothing by
When the weather was warm?" Said the cricket, "Not I.
My heart was so light
That I sang day and night,
For all nature looked gay."
"You sang, sir, you say?
Go then," said the ant, "and dance winter away."
Thus ending, he hastily lifted the wicket
And out of the door turned the poor little cricket.

Test your understanding of the poem. Answer the questions.

1. Why did the cricket complain?
   _____
   _____

2. Why could the cricket not get himself any food during the cold winter months?
   _____
   _____

3. 'Dripping with wet and trembling with cold,' where did the cricket head to?
   _____
   _____

4. Why did the ant not lend any food to the cricket?
   _____
   _____

5. From this fable, what do you learn about the quality of self-discipline? Which character showed and which didn't show self-discipline?
   _____
   _____

More about the value

We are not born with self-discipline. We have to inculcate the habit. Self-discipline is difficult. It is easier, just like it was for the cricket, to give into what we want to do. But not at all times, will this be good for us. For instance, it is fun to play in the rain. However, it is wise to remember that playing in rain could make us sick, and hence we should avoid getting wet in the rain all the time. Those who are able to stay away from getting wet in the rain though it is fun and inviting are those with self-discipline.

Also, self-discipline, as the word suggests is something that has to come from within the self. When we are young, our parents, grandparents or someone older tells us what is good or bad for us. Also, they tell guide us into doing what is good for us. As we grow older, we have to take the responsibility for ourselves. We have to be responsible for our actions.

By showing self-discipline and sticking to what is good for us, and staying away from what is bad for us, we will be able to become healthier and more successful. We will be better citizens. We will be able to make our dreams a reality. Self-discipline gets you what you want.

Research has also shown that people who have self-discipline are happier people.

A VALUE FOR ME
With self-discipline, almost anything is possible.

Snippet

Mansur Ali Khan Pataudi aka Tiger Pataudi was a charismatic prince amongst cricketers. As a 20-year-old, Pataudi lost his right eye due to an accident in England. This was before he played for India. Tiger didn't let this accident affect his dream to play for the country. He practiced batting with one eye and excelled as a cricketer. How do you think a young person, despite having lost one eye, rose to become not merely one of the finest cricketers from India but also the captain for the Indian cricket team? It was his self-discipline. A person with only one eye sees things differently. Try covering one of your eyes. Now look at an object far away. Keep a finger in line with the object that you have singled out. Without moving the finger that you have used to point to the object, close the other eye with the other hand. Now look at the object. Are you surprised to see that your finger and the object are no longer in one line?

Now imagine the kind of practice that Mansur Ali Khan Pataudi had to put in to become the great cricketer that he was.

Let Us Do

1. **Sticking to one's routine requires self-discipline. Also, self-discipline is learnt by sticking to one's routine.**

   For instance, you have learnt that going early to bed and rising early is good for you. It takes great self-discipline to do so every day no matter what day of the year it is.

   Chart out a routine for yourself. This need not necessarily be the one that you follow every day. It should, however, be the one that you want to follow because it is good for you.

Time	Activity

   Make a copy of this routine and stick it at a place that you would see every day. Check if you are able to stick to your routine? If you are able to, you have self-discipline. Else, you need to develop it.

2. **According to you which of the following activities require self-discipline? Tick your answers and cross out the others.**

   a. Waking up early, even on a holiday, because rising early is healthy. ☐

   b. Staying away from junk foods even though you like them. ☐

   c. Getting ready to watch your favourite movie on TV. ☐

d. Dressing up neatly and smartly to school every day. ☐

e. Learning to play a musical instrument. ☐

f. Switching off lights and other electrical gadgets when they are not in use. ☐

g. Writing neatly and legibly. ☐

h. Listening to parents, teachers and other elders. ☐

i. Following rules even when no one is keeping a lookout. ☐

3. No one is perfect. We all strive to be perfect, though. Write down 2-3 of your flaws. How do you plan to overcome them? Keep a track of whether you have been successful at your attempt over the next one week. If you are successful for a week, test your self-discipline by extending the same task for the next one month.

What are my flaws? What do I need to overcome?	Was I successful for a week in my attempt to overcome my flaws?	Was I successful for a month in my attempt to overcome my flaws?

4. Find four other words that are closely related to self-discipline in the word grid below.

D	E	T	E	R	M	I	N	A	T	I	O	N
A	B	K	C	H	O	I	C	E	D	J	F	L
T	U	C	V	B	A	W	I	L	L	R	E	C
G	S	E	L	F	C	O	N	T	R	O	L	Y

5. **Which of the following people show self-discipline? Tick your answers and cross out the others.**

   a. Even when there is no other vehicle at the junction, Mr Rehman always stops if the traffic light turns red. ☐

   b. Madhu, the night watchman never falls asleep during his watch. ☐

   c. Believing the old mansion to be deserted, Sheela empties her dustbins in the mansion's gardens. That way, she avoids walking an additional 100 meters to the municipal dustbin. ☐

   d. Chottu has been told by the doctor not to drink anything cold. The weather is very hot. Chottu wants to drink water from the fridge yet he doesn't. ☐

Are you self-disciplined? Test yourself.
1. Do you eat regularly at fixed timings?
2. Do you eat healthy food?
3. Do you like breaking rules?
4. Do you respond and answer immediately when your parents call you?
5. Do you complete your school work on time without postponing it?
6. Do you get angry very easily and hurt someone else or yourself when you get angry?
7. Do you forgive others?
8. Do you share with others?

   *If your answers to all the above except 3 and 6 are 'yes', then you have tremendous self-discipline. That is great. Keep it going. However, if your answers to those questions were 'no' then you need to work on your self-discipline. Remember, it comes with practice and a conscious effort.

Tips to Parents and Teachers

Teaching children self-discipline takes a lot of effort. It is also a long process. However, by teaching a child to respect himself or herself will help to instill self-discipline. A child with self-respect will be able to easily identify what is good or bad for him/her. Thereby, self-discipline is that much easier.

Also, when children are taught to be responsible for their own actions, they will show greater self-discipline.

Do's and Don'ts

1. Believe and get convinced about what is good for you and what isn't.
2. Follow people who maintain self-discipline.
3. Stay away from those who don't.
4. Try and follow your routine every day.
5. Identify your flaws and bad habits. Make a conscious effort to change for the better.

Valuing Time

Time that has gone by, has gone by forever. It will never come back. Therefore, it is important to learn to value time. It is important to learn to spend time well. It is important to live in such a way that we never feel sorry for not using the past in a better way.

Valuing time is a very important quality for living a better life.

Read the following story to learn more about valuing time.

The Story

There was once a man in China. He was very sad. Nothing was going well for him. Whatever he tried was always a failure. He was so sad with himself and his life that he wanted to end it.

He left his home, parents, wife and children behind in his village and walked into the woods. He started speaking loudly to God "Why is my life so miserable? Why does everything I do turn into a failure? Why don't I ever succeed in anything I do?"

While he was going on and on this way, a voice spoke to him. "You said you wanted to end your life. You said you wanted to quit. Why do you want to quit?" the voice said.

The man looked around and could not see anyone. "Who is it? Who is speaking to me?" he asked.

The voice answered, "It is I, your God. Now, will you tell me why you want to quit? You shouldn't be thinking so."

The man then said, "If you are God, you surely know that I fail at whatever I try. Nothing ever goes right for me. Tell me one reason why I should not quit."

The voice then said, "Look around you. What do you see?"

The man did as the voice demanded and replied, "Ferns and bamboo trees."

"Correct," replied the voice. "I planted them here. I gave them water and light to grow. The fern grew quickly from the earth. Its lovely leaves covered the forest expanse. However, there was nothing at the place where I planted the bamboo. Not a shoot, not a leaf, not a stem."

"In the meantime, the ferns continued to grow and became a beautiful sight to see. I waited patiently. The seasons changed and a year passed by. Still there was nothing from the bamboo. A third year also came and went by and still the bamboo seed was just as it was on the day I had planted it there. Same was the case in the fourth year. There was still no bamboo around."

"It was only in the fifth year that a tiny sprout emerged from the earth. The bamboo seed had finally decided to shoot up. It was very small compared to the lush green expanse of the ferns on the forest floor."

"Six months later, the bamboo rose to over 100 feet in length. There wasn't any mightier and stronger plant in this forest. Now do you understand that some things take time, while some don't. You need to value time, have patience and never give up on life."

Valuing time doesn't necessarily mean doing things in time without wasting it. It also means being able to wait patiently for things to happen in time. Not everything can be hastened. Some things take time.

Test your understanding of the story. Answer the questions.

1. Why was the man from China very sad?
   _____
   _____

2. Why did the man walk into the woods?
   _____
   _____

3. Who spoke to the man in the woods?
   _____
   _____

4. Why do you think the ferns grew fast and the bamboo didn't?
   _____
   _____

5. What do you understand about valuing time from this story?

_____
_____

More about the value

Have you seen an older member in your family, one of your grandparents perhaps, suffering from toothache? Ask him/her how painful it is. Ask whether he/she enjoys having artificial teeth in their mouths instead of their natural ones.

He/ she would tell you that it was because he/she hadn't taken care of their teeth when he/she was younger that they are suffering today. Your grandparent would definitely want to go back to his/her younger days and brush his/her teeth regularly twice daily.

However, going back to the past is an impossibility. Therefore, we should learn to appreciate and value the present. If we take care of our teeth and gums properly brush them twice a day, and eat healthy food while avoiding junk food, we can have strong and healthy teeth even when we become old.

Every day has only a limited number of minutes and hours. This is the same for everyone. However, how is it that some in your class are able to finish their work in time while others are not? Why is it that some are excelling in studies, sports or arts while others aren't? It is not necessarily because they are more talented. It is because they are using those hours of a day to learn something and practice it, to become better at it.

Knowing the importance of time, and using it well will help us become better people; and will help us make our dreams come true.

A VALUE FOR ME
Lost time is never found again.

Snippet

A king of a rich kingdom was friends with a poor man called Hari. He was a good man and fun to be around. However, he was extremely lazy. Therefore, he was also poor.

One day, the king asked Hari, "Why don't you do any work to earn some money? Your wife and children will be better clothed and better fed."

Hari replied, "Who will give me work? Everyone is jealous that I am your friend. So they will not give me work."

The king thought for a while and said, "Since no one will give you work, I offer you access to my treasury only for a day. Go and take as much money you want from it, but you need to do so before sunset. You will never want money anymore. You don't have to work either."

Hari was overjoyed. He decided to go to the treasury that very same day, Hari ran back home to share the news with his wife. His wife said, "Oh this is wonderful indeed. We will be very rich. Go immediately."

"What is the hurry?" Hari said. "Serve me lunch. I will go once I have eaten."

After Hari finished eating, his wife said, "Now go to the treasury. Get back as much money as you can."

"What is the hurry?" Hari said. "I will take a short nap before leaving for the treasury."

And so he went to sleep. However, lazy that he was, he did not feel like getting up from his bed. He slept for quite some time. Finally, he woke up and walked to the royal treasury.

However when he reached the treasury, the guards stopped him from entering. "But I have the king's permission," said Hari.

"We too have orders from the king," replied one of the guards outside the treasury. "You can enter only before sunset. Look up, the sun is setting. So you cannot go in."

Hari went back home as poor as he was that morning. If only he had respect and value for time, he would have been one of the richest people in the kingdom that evening.

Let Us Do

1. **Write down at least three ways in which you value your time.**

   _____
   _____
   _____

   Write down at least three ways in which you value others' time.

   _____
   _____
   _____

2. Somethings take time. Other things need to be done as quickly as possible. Slot the following according to the time they need to be accomplished.

   a. Seeds growing into mighty trees

   b. Completing the day's home work

   c. Training hard so that you can one day become the school football team captain

   d. Pumping air into the cycle tyre on time, before it goes flat

   e. Fixing a leaking tap

Things that take time	Things that should be done immediately

3. All the following proverbs are about time. Fill in the blanks and complete the crossword puzzle.

   Clues:

   1. A _____ in time saves nine.

   2. Yesterday in the past, tomorrow is the future, but today is a gift. That is why is called the _____.

   3. The _____ bird catches the worm.

   4. Rome was not _____ in a day.

   5. Early to bed and early to rise makes you _____, wealthy and wise.

   6. Time and _____ wait for none.

   7. Better three hours too soon than a minute too _____.

4. What are the activities that you would like to do in your free time? Think of at least ten productive ways. Productive ways are those that help you to develop yourself like learning new things or doing something useful.

___
___
___
___
___
___
___
___
___
___
___

5. Who among the following people value time? Tick your answers and cross out the others.

   a. Harry has been advised to practice Yoga every day. This would help him to become a healthier person. He wakes up early every morning. He likes to sit in his balcony and watch the sunrise while sipping his coffee. However, now that he wanted to practice yoga, he decided to cut down his time in the balcony and do yoga instead. ☐

   b. Sarala has a lot of homework to complete. She ought to start doing it immediately after drinking her milk. She however, decides to watch TV for some time and start her work later. After watching TV, she runs out to play with her friends. Later, when she returns home, she sits down to do her work. It is well past her bedtime. She ought to be sleeping; however, she sits up late that night to complete her work. ☐

   c. Mohan is supposed to pick up Mr and Mrs Mehta from the railway station. He was told to be at the station before the train arrives. He started late from home, and got stuck in the traffic jam. Mohan reaches the station half an hour late. ☐

Do you value time? Test yourself.

1. Do you find yourself doing things at the last minute?
2. Do you complete your tasks well in time?
3. Do you make a list of things that need to be done and see which task is more important than the other?
4. Do you stop working and take a break whenever you feel like it?
5. Do you believe in completing your work before relaxing or enjoying yourself?

   *If your answers to the questions 2, 3 and 5 have been 'yes' then you definitely value time. If not, then you need to understand that time and tide wait for not. Learn to make the best use of time. Only when you have completed your task in time, you will have time to enjoy yourself better.

Tips to Parents and Teachers

Help children to chalk out a timetable for themselves. Help them to stick to their timetable. Lessons taught early in life stick with them for a longer time. Teach them that leisure time ought to come after time well spent in a productive activity. That way, they will be able to enjoy their leisure freely and without any guilt.

They will also turn out to be more responsible children and adults.

Do's and Don'ts

1. Value every second.
2. Play while you play and read while you read. That way you will be doing justice to what you are doing and to yourself.
3. While waiting for a bus or standing in a queue, you could use the free time on hand to complete some work. For instance, you could make a note of the things that you need to do that day.
4. Never postpone things if you can help it. Finish what needs to be done as soon as possible.
5. Be organized. Keep things where they belong to. That way you will be saving time when you have to fetch them again. Else, you will waste time searching for them.
6. Take time off to rest. Rest is as important as exercise.
7. Do everything for the right amount of time. For instance, if you need to sleep for 8 hours, do so. You should not sleep less or more. Either way, your body will not feel good and well rested. In the same way, if you have to play for two hours, do so. However, if you play for a long time, your body will get exhausted and will not leave you fit to play even for those two hours in the following few days.

A Collage of Values

Make a collage of the various kinds of values displayed by people. For instance, you could paste a newspaper clipping about an act of courage and bravery.

Use the space here to make your collage.

Sympathy

When you see someone crying, do you feel sad? Do you feel like crying yourself? This feeling is called sympathy. Sympathy is the feelings of pity and sorrow we experience for someone else's unhappiness and grief.

Sympathy is a good quality. It helps you to feel for others. It helps you to think about others.

Read the following story to learn more about the value of sympathy.

Story

Once there were two friends who were walking on a deserted road. They saw a farmer working in his fields alone. They also noticed a pair of old and frayed shoes on the road. They assumed that the shoes belonged to the farmer.

One of the boys was bored and declared, "I am going to do something funny. I will remove the shoes from here and hide them somewhere else. We can hide behind that bush by the side of the road, and watch the owner of the shoes search for them. It will be fun."

It so happened that one of their teachers was passing by that very road. He overheard the boy's plan. He came over to the boys and said, "We should never amuse ourselves at the cost of hurting someone. I have a better plan. Instead of hiding the person's shoes, why don't you place some money in each of his shoes and see what happens? I can assure you that you will be stunned and pleased with the result."

The boy did as his teacher said. He placed some money in both the shoes. He, his friend and the teacher then went and hid behind the bushes they had spotted earlier.

After a while, the farmer, having finished his work in the field, washed himself in the nearby stream and walked to where he had kept his shoes. When he slipped on his shoes, he naturally found something pressed between his feet and the shoes. He bent down to check what was in the shoes.

To his astonishment, he found money in them. He looked around but could see no one. He did not know who had kept money in his shoes, but he was glad for the kind gesture. He was so moved by it, that he could no longer contain his emotions.

His eyes filled with tears of

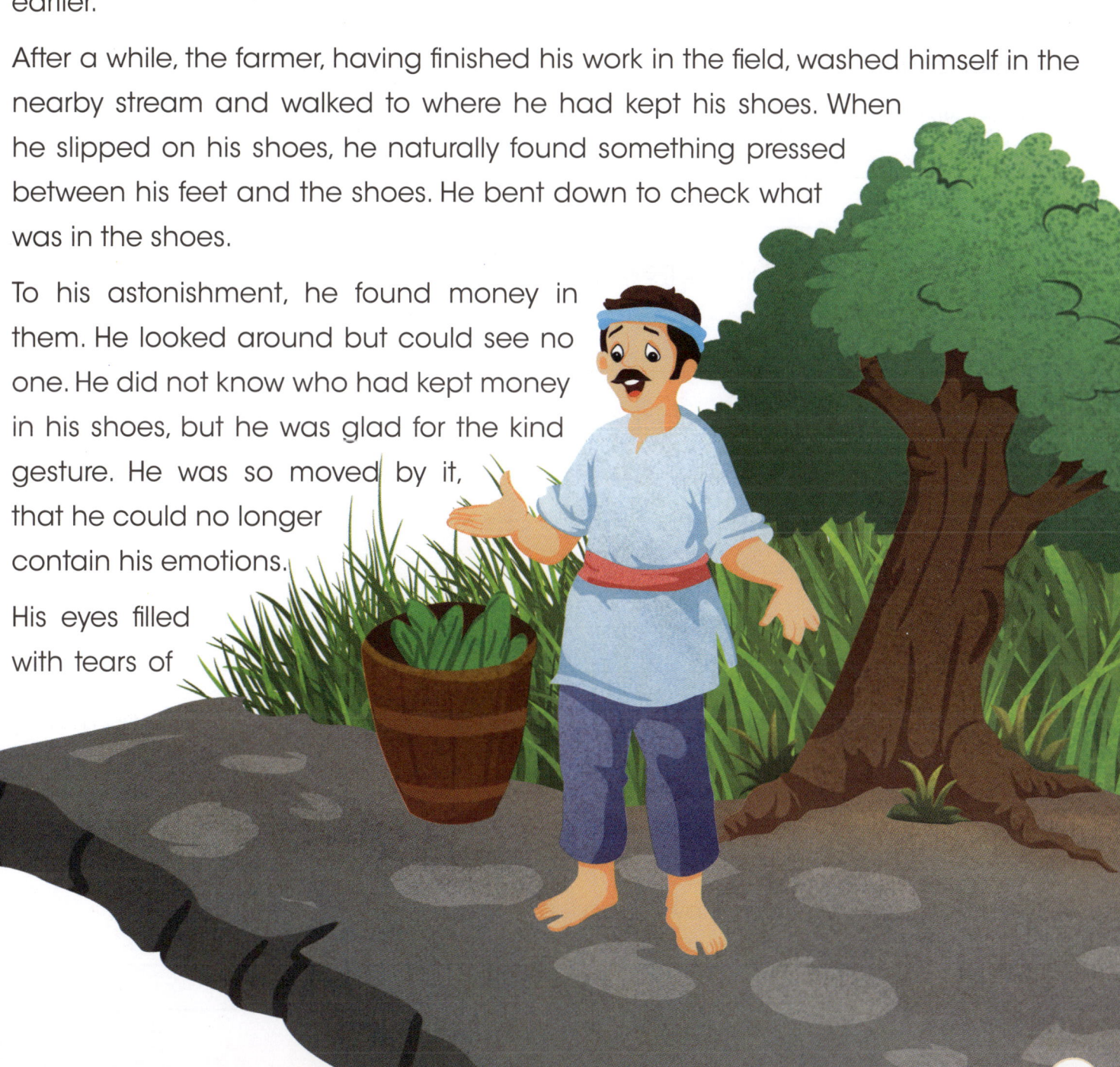

joy. He said aloud, "I am not sure who has done this, but your kind gesture done out of sympathy will help me immensely. I will be able to buy medicines for my sick wife and some food for my children. I have been working hard for extra hours for the money, and now I have received help without knowing who has helped me. I don't have words to thank you."

The boy hiding behind the bush along with his friend and the teacher were stunned. He turned to his teacher and said, "I had no idea how a little money would mean so much to the poor man. What you suggested has indeed opened my eyes. There is pleasure in giving and sharing. It feels so good to help and show sympathy towards others."

Test your understanding of the story. Answer the questions.

1. What did the boy notice in the field?

2. Whom did the frayed shoes belong to?

3. Why did the boy want to hide the shoes?

4. What did the teacher suggest instead?

5. Why was the farmer moved when he realised that someone had placed money in his shoes?

6. What do you understand by the value of sympathy from this story?

More about the value

As we have read above, sympathy is a good quality. It helps us to feel for and think about others. It helps you to behave in such a way that you do not intentionally harm or hurt others.

Don't you feel good to have friends around you when you fall off your cycle? They would come running to you, help you up on your feet, lift your cycle, check for any damages to the cycle, and run up to your parents to inform them that you are hurt.

This is an act done out of sympathy. On the contrary, would you like others to stand by and watch while you pick yourself and your cycle up and limp all the way back to your house, only to find your parents busy with their work and not spare even a glance at you?

It is not merely sufficient to feel sympathy. An action should follow. Often times, a good kind word is enough to make the other person feel better. At other times, some kind of help will help the poor person in his/her bad times.

A VALUE FOR ME

Shared joy is a double joy; shared sorrow is half a sorrow.

Snippet

There is a story told in the southern part of our country of a truthful cow and a merciful tiger. The tiger, they say was an old one. It found hunting for the fast sprinting deer very difficult. It so resorted to attacking grazing sheep and cows. They were after all slower animals and easier to prey upon.

One evening, just as the cows of a herd were returning to their village and to the safety of their sheds, the tiger pounced on them from some rocks where it was hiding. It managed to catch hold of a cow. The rest of the cattle ran back to the village.

Just as the tiger was about to kill and eat the cow, the cow begged the tiger. "O tiger, I do understand that you caught me and hence I am your food now. But I beg you to please let me return once to my home. I have a young calf, who is eagerly waiting for me. It needs me for my milk. I will feed him one last time, tell him how to behave itself when I am no longer with him anymore, and return to you once the task is done."

Though the tiger was a wild and ferocious animal, incapable of pity, yet the sad cow melted the tiger's heart and it allowed the cow to return home for the last time. He warned the cow to return soon, else the consequences would be bad.

The cow went away, glad to be able to see its baby for one last time. The tiger did not expect the cow to return. Yet it was hopeful for its meal. It was indeed surprised to see the cow return after a while. It could also hear the miserable calf whining for its mother. Yet, the cow walked towards the tiger with determination.

The tiger was so by the cow's truthfulness and its calf's misery, that the tiger let the cow return to the village unharmed.

The tiger went away hungry but happy. Sympathy was something that the tiger had never shown earlier but he realised that with sympathy came happiness and contentment.

Let Us Do

1. **You are at the school ground running around the football ground. Your best friend falls. He is not hurt, but his dress is now dirty. Your whole class is laughing because the way he fell was quite comical. What will you do?**

   _____
   _____
   _____
   _____

   Do your actions show that you are a sympathetic person?
   Yes/No

2. **Which of the following fictional characters are sympathetic?**

   a. Seven dwarfs are sympathetic to Snow White's plight.

   True   False

   b. The witch is sympathetic towards Rapunzel and hence locks her up in the tower.

   True   False

   c. Harry Potter is sympathetic towards Ron when he offers to buy several sweets and share.

   True   False

   d. The man who gives Jack from Jack and the Beanstalk the magic beans is sympathetic towards Jack.

   True   False

   e. In the story where the rabbit tricks the lion into jumping into the well when it sees its reflection, the rabbit was sympathetic towards the lion.

   True   False

   f. Heidi brings back the softest of breads for her friend's grandmother, because she was sympathetic.

   True   False

3. **Look at the following emoticons. Write down what each of them means. Imagine a situation where a person would feel these emotions.**

   a. _____

   b. _____

   c. _____

d. _____

e. _____

f. _____

4. Complete the following dialogue between Sharada and Yuvana. Use appropriate expressions to show sympathy.

> okay, sorry, gets well, hope, thank you, sorry, understand, sweet

Sharada: Yuvana, I am here to invite you to my birthday party tomorrow evening.

Yuvana: Oh! How lovely, is it your birthday tomorrow? I would love to come, but I cannot, _____.

Sharada: Why is that so? I hope everything is _____.

Yuvana: No, my brother met with an accident.

Sharada: That is so terrible. I am _____. Is he in much pain?

Yuvana: The medicines have helped ease the pain. But I have to be around him to talk to him, play with him or read books for him.

Sharada: That is so _____ of you. He must be bored without you around.

Yuvana: Yes, I _____ you understand why I cannot come for your party tomorrow.

Sharada: I completely _____. I would like to come over someday if that is fine. We will play an indoor game to make your brother feel better.

Yuvana: That would be so nice, _____. My best wishes to you on your birthday.

Sharada: Thank you Yuvana. Please pass on my regards to your parents. I hope that your brother _____ soon.

5. Sometimes, we realize that the other person is going through a hard time or is in pain. Though we want to help them, we hesitate. Later, we feel terrible for not offering a kind word or for not helping. Did that ever happen to you? Were you always there for your friends and family?

   Be honest and answer the following questions.

   What did you do when you realized that

   a. One of your friends forgot to get his lunch box.
   _____

   b. One of your friends lost a pet.
   _____

   c. One of your friends grandparent passed away.
   _____

   d. One of your friends fell sick.
   _____

   e. One of your friends did not do well in an exam.
   _____

Are you sympathetic? Test yourself.

1. When someone falls down, what do you do?
   a. Laugh ☐   b. help him up ☐
2. When you see a person with a red nose, what comes to your mind?
   a. Cold ☐   b. Clown ☐
3. When one of your classmates forgets his or her lunch, what do you do?
   a. Share your food with that person ☐
   b. Tell that person that they ought to be more careful in the future ☐
   * If all your answers are 'a' then you are a sympathetic person.

Tips to Parents and Teachers

Teach a child to think from another's perspective. Every coin has two sides. Every situation can be seen from several perspectives. While a child may be directly involved in a situation and sees it from his or her perspective, the child should also be able to view it from the others' perspective.

This ability, while teaching sympathy, also leads to resolution of several conflicts. Children are known to be sympathetic when their own emotional needs are met.

Do's and Don'ts

1. Always listen to people. When you listen to them, you can understand their feelings. You can understand what they are going through.

2. Help whenever you can. When you are not in a position to help, stick around your friends nevertheless. Just by being with them shows that you are sympathetic.

3. Never offer advice without first listening to what they have to say.

4. Never say that your own problems are greater than someone else's.

5. Offer a kind word but don't force the other person to follow your advice. Let the person choose for himself or herself.

My Declaration

I promise to _____
_____
_____
_____
_____
_____
_____
_____
_____
_____
_____

Fill in the blanks. All the words that you need are in the word grid.

1. When you have feelings of sorrow or pain for another person's misery or misfortune, you are _____.

S												

3. _____ and tide wait for none.

T			

4. We have an opportunity to gain _____ in every situation.

K									

5. Without a sense of _____ there can be no society.

C					

6. We should treat _____ property with the same care we treat our own property.

N								

7. Self-discipline helps us to _____ almost anything.

A						

8. Knowledge is _____.

P				

9. Justice is being _____ and impartial.

F			

10. Justice is being _____ and impartial.

C										

S	U	C	C	E	S	S	F	U	L	
			C	C	A	R	E			E
K			H							C
N	A	T	I	O	N	A	L			U
O			E							L
W			V					P		A
L			E					O		R
E					F			W		T
D	S	Y	M	P	A	T	H	E	T	I	C
G					I			R		M
E					R					E

56